THE A-LIST

—— CHEF ADRIANNE'S FINEST ——

VOLUME I

Published by Maximum Flavor, Inc.

ISBN 978-0-9909716-6-5

First Printing 2018
Copyright Maximum Flavor, Inc. © 2018
All rights reserved

Author: 37 Calvo
With Sheehan Planas-Arteaga
Executive Producer: Michael Beovides
Food Photography: Erick Coego
Back Cover Photo: Alain Martinez
Design by: Erick Coego

Printed in the United States

Without limiting the rights under copyright reserved above, no part of this publication may be reproduced, stored in or introduced into a retrieval, or transmitted, in any form, or by any means [electronic, mechanical, photocopying, recording, or otherwise], without the prior written permission of both the copyright owner and the above publisher of the book. The scanning, uploading and distribution of this book via any other means without the permission of the publisher is illegal and punishable by law. Please purchase only authorized electronic editions, and do not participate in or encourage electronic piracy of copyrighted materials. Your support of the author's rights is appreciated.

Publisher's Note
The recipes contained in this book are to be followed exactly as written. The publisher is not responsible for your specific health or allergy needs that may require medical supervision. The publisher is not responsible for any adverse reactions to the recipes contained in this book.

Publisher does not have any control over and does not assume any responsibility for author or third-party Web sites on their content.

facebook.com/chefadrianne
twitter.com/chefadrianne
instagram.com/chefadrianne
chefadriannes.com
adriannecalvo.com
makeitcountcharities.org

The B List is not a thing

—Chef Adrianne

"I thank God every day for all the undeserved blessings in my life. One of the greatest blessings is being able to share my love for cooking with everyone, and one that I don't take for granted - not even for a second. This book is dedicated to all those who've helped me, who've impacted me, and who have nurtured my craft. Thank you for standing by me, and with me.
Let the good times roll!"

A

content

I. Introduction

    What Inspires Me? — **8**

II. The A-List

    i. Starters — **14**

        a. Veg Forward — **54**

    ii. Beef & Chops — **110**

    iii. Desserts — **162**

    iv. Fundamentals — **198**

WHAT INSPIRES ME?

Why is it that I do what I do? It is a simple-enough question isn't it? What is it that gets me up in the morning as the warm bed begs me to retreat? What is it that keeps me going when times are tough, as they inevitably are at times? My passion is one that requires complete dedication and a willingness to fail, and fail often. There must be something special that drives me to immerse myself in the world of food every single day. It turns out, this question has a multi-faceted answer.

I have always loved food. Growing up in a Cuban household, shared meals were a very important part of our daily family interaction. To put it lightly; Cubans like to eat. With my mother being the driving force, each day featured a different culinary masterpiece whipped up in our kitchen. I took to it immediately. I was the girl that was obsessed with her Easy Bake Oven, as opposed to her Barbie Dolls. There is no feeling quite like cooking up a meal that delights a guest, and this emotion clung to me since I was standing on my tippy toes to see what was on the stove. For these reasons, family and upbringing were my first motivation to pursue a career as a chef.

Food stirs up certain emotions that few other things in this world can reach. It is more than just the fuel we use to keep our bodies going every day. If it was simply like gasoline in a car, people would not travel from all the ends of the Earth just to try something specific. If it was like water to a plant, people would not document their most memorable meals for all to see (#foodie). If it was like wood in a fire, people would not put their bodies through such strenuous exercise just to be able to eat the delicious foods we all love. For that is one of the most interesting things about food; everyone loves it!

Food has the potential to be the common denominator between even the greatest of enemies. What better way to bring together two parties than with a meal that they can both enjoy? Does melted cheese not also melt even the coldest of hearts? Food is one of the great bridges between people, regardless of where they are from or where they are going. It can connect you to another person's culture, traditions, and history in a way few other things can. A perfect bite can transport the mind to the rivers of Venice, or to the cobblestone streets of New Orleans. Who wouldn't want a piece of that?

The emotional, cultural, and social power of food has always fascinated me, and it is another reason I do what I do today. Each of my dishes is meant to be an experience for the eater, not just a way to quell hunger. If I can take my guests' taste buds for a ride to some remote and beautiful place across an ocean, then I have successfully done the work I love to do. Luckily, my wonderful and loyal fans do not shy away from showing their appreciation, which leads me to one of the most motivating factors behind my work... #loveletterstoachef

#loveletterstoachef is an Instagram hashtag that I started in order to showcase a unique and marvelous aspect of my job. My patrons have been visiting my restaurant for a decade now, as Chef Adrianne's opened in 2007. Since that time, certain guests who particularly enjoyed my meals have taken it upon themselves to not only rave about the restaurant, but to write a note to me and my amazing staff on their receipts! These "love letters," as I have dubbed them, have deeply inspired me to continue improving as a chef.

There is something special about the written word, especially when it is in the form of a "love letter." It takes time, it takes thought, and it is composed with a person's distinct penmanship style. This makes it truly personalized and emotional, which is why film, literature, and theater are littered with stories surrounding letters of affection. The hopeless romantic pours his or her heart and soul onto the page with each swift stroke of the pen, showering the other person with pools of praise. It is a concept that anyone who has ever been in love can surely relate to.

Believe it or not, delicious food can give someone a similar feeling to being in love. A good meal causes the brain to release endorphins that put a person in a euphoric state, not unlike feeling a loving connection towards someone. As a result, this euphoria of the mind is part of my job as a chef. I must take my patrons' palates to a place they have never been before, in order to encounter the lovely feelings we are ever so fond of. If I can successfully transmit pure bliss through the enjoyment of a meal, then maybe, just maybe, my guests can enjoy a little slice of love when they finish dining at Chef Adrianne's. That, it turns out, has become my own personal euphoria.

My #loveletterstoachef postings have varied greatly. From anniversaries, to birthdays, to graduations, to just an ordinary date night, my guests have penned notes to me and my staff on many different types of occasions. Here are just a few of the impactful love letters that we have received at Chef Adrianne's...

"I wanted to just take a moment to thank you for this evening. I have a few medical difficulties that limit what I can eat when they are flaring...I have put aside almost two years of celebration dinners in order to be able to celebrate at this restaurant...It was everything I had dreamed of and more..."
-Cristina

"You made our 2-year anniversary so special! The preparation, quality, and service made our night magical!"
-Alex + Krystel

"I started coming here at age 13...and I will now be turning 22 years old...The only request I have is to please make this delicious guinea pig shrimp + soup for my birthday...which I proudly celebrate with you every year for the past 9 years..."
-Jackie

"Best place to celebrate 2 years cancer free! Food was exceptional as always."
-Anonymous

"Chef, I feel like these love notes will one day be continued by my son! 8 months in now & still, coming here has been the sweetest dates with me & the bump!...will be back for my last meal pre-baby!"
-Chanti

"In life, there are good days, there are bad days, and then there are days that make everything worth it. Those are the great days. Today, chef, was a great day."
-Samantha

It is nearly impossible to describe the feeling my staff and I experience after discovering a love letter written on one of our receipts. Food is a simple thing. And yet, it has the power to help a person overcome an obstacle, or create a positive, life-long memory for an entire group of people. As a chef, there is no greater honor than to be able to positively affect someone's life through a meal at my restaurant. These love letters will always push me to get on my feet every morning, for they are a constant reminder of the influence my work can have.

These recipes are the result of all of this inspiration. From my upbringing, to the conceptual power of food, to the "love letters" my guests have written to me, I can truly say that my motivation has not and will not run dry. Now, you too can ignite the blissful emotions in your guests with these delicious meals. You know why it is I do what I do. With The A-List, you can now learn how.

Chef Adrianne's Vineyard restaurant
11510 SW 147th Ave
Miami FL 33196
305-408-8386
www.Chefadriannes.com

Sale
20180626-10042   Station ID : 11
                                Marcelo

Amazing food!!

Chef Adrianne's Vineyard restaurant
11510 SW 147th Ave
Miami FL 33196
305-408-8386
www.Chefadriannes.com

Sale   Station ID : 11
                                Bruce

Making Mother's Day extra Special!! Always a pleasure dining with you guys!! :)
Ulises & Shannon Wiltz

Chef A
Thank you for another amazing ___. We come monthly for ___

Once again celebrating anniversary best wa___

Thanks chef for a remarkable 32nd anniversary dinner. Where come from they call people like you Monstro
Thanks
J.

...experience... ...ted it's ...GOD. PORN" ...ha feel forever ...my heart
Irene

Thank you for allowing us ___ enjoy your food!

brown sugar crusted italian sausage — 16

bacon, egg, and charred brussels — 19

crispy braised pork belly — 22

buttery sausage, egg, and cheese kische casserole — 25

sweet potato skins — 28

poached egg crostini — 33

green chile chicken empanadas — 37

pork bao al pastor — 41

grilled focaccia — 44

foie gras and mortadella bruschetta — 47

sweet corn arepas — 49

blueberry, ham, and swiss on brioche — 52

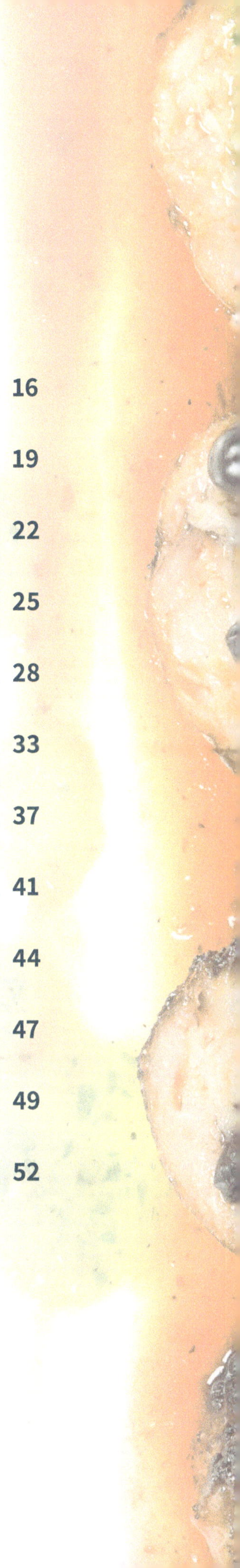

brown sugar crusted italian sausage
with blackberry cucumber relish

Serves: 2

INGREDIENTS:

- 2 spicy Italian links
- 1 tablespoon brown sugar
- 1 tablespoon canola oil
- ½ cup blackberries, chopped
- ¼ cup cucumber, chopped
- 1 teaspoon red onion, minced
- 1 teaspoon lemon juice
- 1 teaspoon honey
- 1 teaspoon cilantro, minced
- pinch Kosher salt

DIRECTIONS:

In a large sauté pan, heat up the canola oil to medium high. Rub the sausage links with brown sugar and place in the sauté pan. Cook on medium high heat, rolling to brown on each side.

Cook for 8-10 minutes or until cooked through. Set aside.

For the relish, add blackberries, cucumber, onion, lemon juice, honey, cilantro, and salt to a small mixing bowl. Set aside.

To serve, slice the sausage into ½" thick pieces. Align on a serving dish and top with a spoonful of relish onto each slice of sausage.

bacon, egg, and charred brussels

Serves: 2

INGREDIENTS:

- 1 cup Brussels sprouts, halved
- 1 tablespoon melted butter, unsalted
- 1 tablespoon light soy sauce
- 1 teaspoon garlic, minced
- ¼ teaspoon crushed red pepper flakes
- ¼ cup applewood smoked bacon, chopped
- 1 tablespoon maple syrup
- 1 teaspoon white distilled vinegar
- 2 eggs poached
- chives, minced for garnish

DIRECTIONS:

Preheat the oven to 400 degrees F. In a mixing bowl, combine melted butter, soy sauce, garlic, and red pepper. Add the Brussels sprouts and toss to coat evenly.

Place on a cookie sheet and bake for 12-15 minutes or until they begin to slightly char. At the same time, toss chopped bacon and maple syrup together and place on a cookie sheet.

Bake for 13-15 minutes. Meanwhile, bring a small pot of water to a boil with a teaspoon of vinegar. Lower heat to a simmer and gently drop each egg into the simmering water.

Using a wooden spoon, stir slowly. After 2-3 minutes of simmering, remove the eggs one at a time, onto a plate.

Toss bacon and Brussels sprouts together, and place onto the center of a plate. Top with poached egg and chopped chives as garnish.

crispy braised pork belly

with pickled sweet peppers and garlic cilantro aioli

Serves: 4

INGREDIENTS:

- 1 lb pork belly, skinless
- ½ cup light soy sauce
- ½ cup water
- 1 tablespoon garlic, minced
- ¼ cup sweet chili
- ½ cup white vinegar
- 1 teaspoon sesame oil
- 1 cup sweet peppers, thinly sliced
- 1 cup sugar
- 1 cup white vinegar
- ½ cup cilantro
- 1 tablespoon garlic, minced
- 1 tablespoon lime juice
- 1 tablespoon honey
- ½ cup mayonnaise
- Kosher salt and pepper, to taste
- cilantro, flash fried for garnish

DIRECTIONS:

Preheat the oven to 350 degrees F. In a mixing bowl, whisk together soy sauce, water, garlic, sweet chili, vinegar, and sesame oil. Place pork belly in a baking dish and pour mixture over it. Cover with aluminum foil and bake for 2.5 hours or until fork tender.

Meanwhile, place sweet peppers, sugar, and vinegar in a small pot. Cook over medium heat for 15 minutes or until vinegar is reduced by half. Set aside. In a food processor, add cilantro, garlic, lime juice, and honey. Pulse a few times until well combined.

Add mixture to a small bowl and add mayonnaise. Whisk together and season to taste with salt and pepper. Preheat a fryer or pot with canola oil to 375 degrees F. Place the cooked pork belly in fryer for 30 seconds or until edges crisp up. Also, flash fry a handful of cilantro for garnish.

To plate, place a spoonful of garlic cilantro aioli in center of plate. Add the crispy pork belly and top with pickled sweet peppers and crispy cilantro.

Note:

The garlic cilantro aioli is highly addictive and pairs well with almost any protein. It stores well for days in the fridge so I always make extra to keep around!

buttery sausage, egg, and cheese kische casserole

with maple syrup tomato

Serves: 8-10

INGREDIENTS:

- 7 croissants, rough chopped
- 1 tablespoon butter, more for baking dish
- ¼ cup green onions, chopped
- 1 lb andouille sausage, chopped
- ½ cup breakfast sausage, sliced
- ½ cup bacon, crisped, chopped
- ½ cup red bell pepper, finely chopped
- ½ cup yellow onion, finely chopped
- 8 large eggs
- 3 cups whole milk
- 1 cup heavy cream
- 2 cups pepperjack cheese, grated
- Kosher salt and pepper, to taste
- ½ cup maple syrup

DIRECTIONS:

Preheat the oven to 350 degrees F. Heat a large skillet to medium high heat. Add butter and sauté green onions, sausages, and bacon for 3-4 minutes. Add bell peppers and onions.
Cook for another 3-4 minutes. Set aside. In a large bowl, whisk together eggs, milk, and heavy cream.
Add croissants and sautéed mixture. Add shredded cheese and season to taste with salt and pepper.
Grease an 8x8 baking dish and pour mixture into it. Bake for 35-45 minutes. Allow to cool. To serve, drizzle with maple syrup.

sweet potato skins
with spanish chorizo and pickled onons

Serves: 2

INGREDIENTS:

- 2 medium sweet potatoes
- ¼ cup heavy cream
- Kosher salt and freshly ground pepper to taste
- 1 tablespoon extra virgin olive oil
- ¼ cup yellow onion, minced
- ½ teaspoon garlic, minced
- ¼ Spanish chorizo, minced
- pinch crushed red pepper flakes
- ¼ cup light beer
- 1 teaspoon green onion, thinly sliced
- ½ cup shredded mozzarella
- 1 tablespoon sour cream
- 1 small red onion, thinly sliced
- ½ cup red wine vinegar
- pinch dried oregano

DIRECTIONS:

Preheat the oven to 400 degrees F. Pierce each sweet potato a few times and bake on cookie sheet for 40-50 minutes or until soft. Allow the potatoes to cool slightly. Slice potatoes in half lengthwise.

Reduce oven temperature to 375 degrees F. Scoop out sweet potato flesh, leaving a thin layer of sweet potato inside, and add flesh to a medium bowl. Place skins back on the baking sheet face up, drizzle with olive oil and bake for 8-10 minutes.

Mash the sweet potato flesh with heavy cream, salt, and pepper until smooth and creamy. Set aside. Meanwhile, in a sauté pan, heat the olive oil to medium high heat. Add the onion, garlic, and chorizo. Sauté and stir for 5-7 minutes. Add the red pepper flakes. Cook for another minute or so. Add the beer to deglaze the pan. Add the green onions and remove from the heat.

Set aside. In a small pot, add the sliced red onion, vinegar, and oregano. Bring to a simmer and then turn off the heat. Set aside. Remove the skins from the oven.

To assemble, fill each potato skin with the mashed sweet potato, then add the chorizo mixture. Top with mozzarella cheese and bake for 3-5 minutes or until cheese melts. Remove from the oven and top with a dollop of sour cream and finish with pickled onion.

poached egg crostini
with prosciutto and provolone

Serves: 2

INGREDIENTS:

- 2 slices Italian bread
- 1 garlic clove, smashed
- 1 tablespoon butter
- ¼ teaspoon dried parsley
- 2 eggs
- 1 tablespoon white vinegar
- 4 slices prosciutto
- 2 slices provolone cheese
- 1 cup baby arugula
- 1 tablespoon extra virgin olive oil
- 1 teaspoon champagne vinegar
- Kosher salt and pepper
- 1 tablespoon Parmesan shavings

DIRECTIONS:

Preheat the oven to 400 degrees F. In a wide pan, add butter and garlic. Cook over medium heat for 30 seconds.

Press the bread slices onto the buttered pan and cook for one minute. Place onto a baking sheet. Place a slice of provolone on each buttered bread and sprinkle with dried parsley.

Bake in oven for five minutes or until cheese melts. Meanwhile bring a small pot of water to a simmer with a spoonful of vinegar.

Carefully drop each egg into simmering water and gently swirl around until the egg white starts to film. Poach for approximately 90 seconds to two minutes. Using a slotted spoon, remove eggs from water and set aside.

Place two prosciutto slices on each crostini. Toss baby arugula in champagne vinegar and olive oil. Season with Kosher salt and pepper to taste. Place a poached egg on each crostini and add tossed arugula. Add Parmesan shaving to finish.

green chile chicken empanadas

with cabbage slaw

Serves: 5

INGREDIENTS:

- 4 medium tomatillos, husked and rinsed
- 1 jalapeño, seeded and deveined
- 1 yellow onion, quartered
- 5 garlic cloves, smashed
- 1 cup cilantro leaves, chopped
- 1 lime, juiced
- ¼ cup water
- ½ teaspoon Kosher salt
- 1 cup chicken, cooked and shredded
- 1 cup crumbled queso fresco
- 1 large egg beaten for egg wash
- butter, for greasing the pans
- 1 cup cabbage, shredded
- 1 tablespoon red wine vinegar
- 1 tablespoon extra virgin olive oil

EMPANADA DOUGH:

- water
- 1 ½ cups all-purpose flour
- 1 cup masa harina
- 1 teaspoon baking powder
- 1 teaspoon Kosher salt
- ½ cup unsalted butter, melted

DIRECTIONS:
Bring a pot of water to a boil and add the tomatillos, jalapeño, onion, and garlic. Simmer for 10 to 15 minutes until the tomatillos are soft. Drain. Combine the tomatillos, jalapeño, onion, garlic, cilantro, and lime juice in a blender. Add water and pulse. Add salt and pulse again. Combine the shredded chicken and queso fresco in a large mixing bowl. Pour in 1 ½ cups of the salsa verde and fold the ingredients together to moisten. Use as a filling for empanadas.

EMPANADA DOUGH:
In a large bowl, sift together the flour, masa harina, baking powder, and salt. Stir in butter. Add ½ cup to ¾ cup of water, working it in with your hands. Form the dough into a ball, wrap it in plastic, and chill for 30 minutes.
Lightly flour your rolling pin and counter. Divide the dough in half and roll it out to 1/8" thickness. Using a 4" cookie or biscuit cutter, cut out ten circles of dough. Spoon two generous tablespoons of filling into the center of each dough circle, leaving a ½" border. Brush the edges with the egg wash and then fold the dough to enclose the filling and form a semi-circle. Tightly seal the edges by crimping with a fork. Preheat the oven to 375 degrees F. Place the empanadas on a buttered baking sheet and brush the tops with additional egg wash. Using a fork, prick the top of the empanadas for steam to escape.
Bake for 30 minutes. Serve on top of slaw.

pork bao al pastor
with chipotle ranch

Serves: 2

INGREDIENTS:

- 3 steam buns (bao buns)
- ¼ lb pork tenderloin, trimmed
- 1 tablespoon garlic, minced
- 1 tablespoon light soy sauce
- 1 tablespoon brown sugar
- 1 tablespoon canola oil
- ¼ cup pineapple, minced
- 1 tablespoon cilantro, minced
- 1 teaspoon red onion, minced
- ½ teaspoon jalapeño, seeded and minced
- 1 teaspoon lime juice
- pinch Kosher salt
- 1 tablespoon chipotle sauce
- 1 tablespoon mayonnaise
- 1 teaspoon ranch seasoning
- sliced cucumber
- sliced Fresno chili
- sliced radish

DIRECTIONS:

On a clean work surface, slice the pork into ¼" thick slices. Mix together garlic, soy sauce, and brown sugar. Cover pork in the mixture and refrigerate for 3-4 hours.

Using a steamer, steam buns for 15-20 minutes. Set aside. In a hot skillet with canola oil, cook pork over medium heat 5-7 minutes.

Set aside. In a small mixing bowl, combine pineapple, cilantro, onion, jalapeño, lime, and salt. Set aside. In another small mixing bowl, whisk together chipotle, mayonnaise, and ranch. To assemble, place a couple of cooked slices of pork into each bao bun, then top with pineapple salsa. Add slices of cucumber, chili, and radish. Finish with a drizzle of chipotle ranch.

INGREDIENTS:

- 4 small squares focaccia bread
- 1 teaspoon extra virgin olive oil
- 1 garlic clove
- 1 piece burrata mozzarella cheese, quartered
- sea salt, to taste
- 1 teaspoon pink peppercorns, crushed
- 1 teaspoon white truffle oil
- 1 tablespoon honey
- chives, minced, for garnish

DIRECTIONS:

Preheat he oven to 400 degrees F.
Place the focaccia squares on a cookie sheet, rub each one with the garlic clove, and drizzle with olive oil.
Bake for ten minutes. Meanwhile, in a small bowl, mix together the honey and truffle. Set aside.
To assemble, place a quarter of the burrata cheese on top of each toasted focaccia.
Sprinkle with sea salt. Drizzle with truffle honey, and add crushed pink peppercorns. Garnish with minced chives.

grilled focaccia
with burrata cheese, crushed pink peppercorns, and truffle honey

Serves: 2

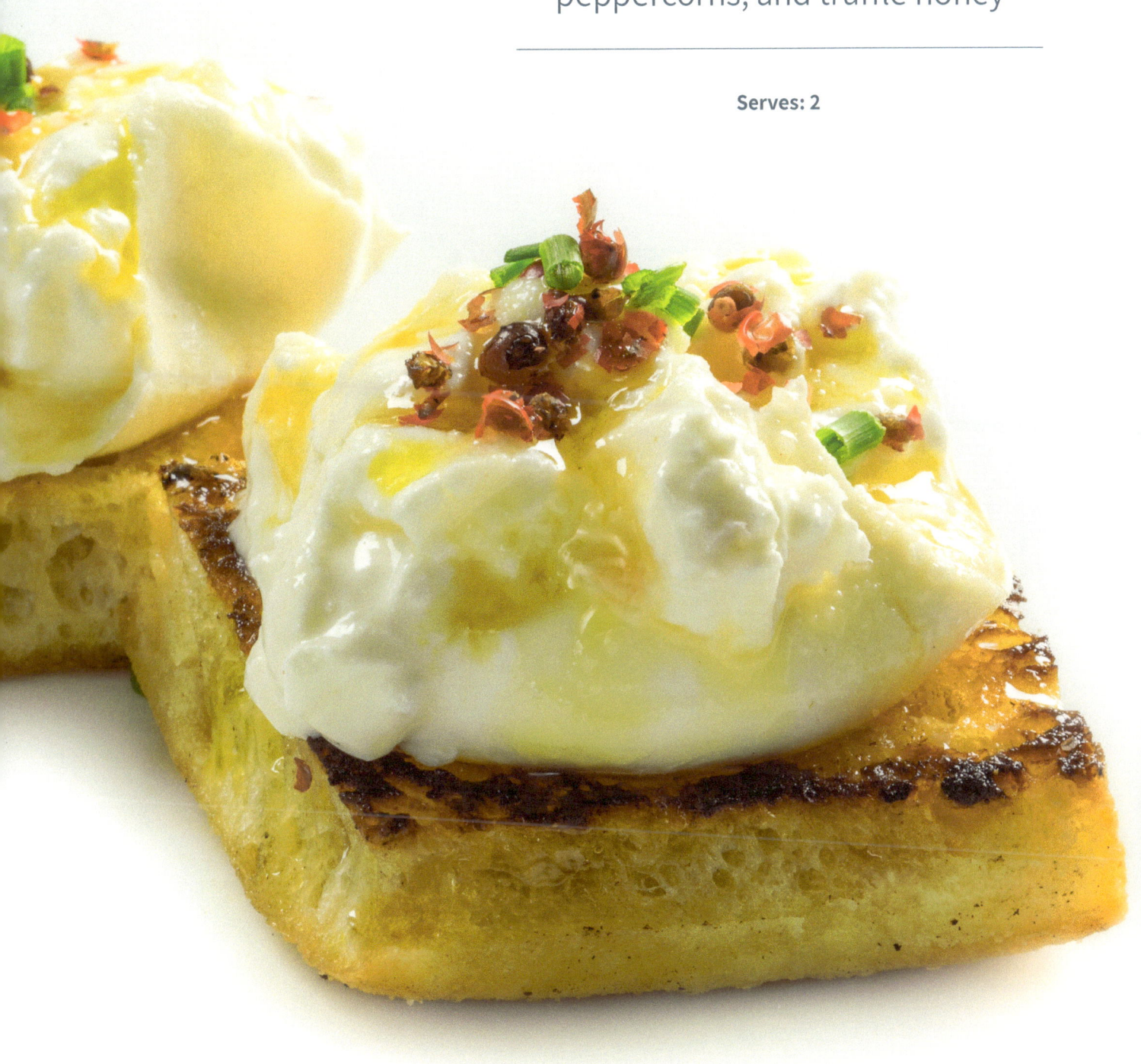

foie gras and mortadella bruschetta

Serves: 2

INGREDIENTS:

- 4   2" pieces ciabatta bread, toasted
- 1   tablespoon Dijon mustard
- 4   slices mortadella, thinly sliced
- ¼   lb foie gras, trimmed and cut into squares
- 1   tablespoon canola oil
- 1   tablespoon cornichons, minced
- 1   teaspoon white truffle oil chives, minced for garnish whole grain mustard, smear for garnish

DIRECTIONS:

Heat canola oil in a small sauté pan to medium high heat.

Add the foie gras and cook 2-3 minutes on each side. Set aside.

Spread Dijon mustard on each toasted ciabatta square and top with a slice of mortadella. Add a piece of foie gras.

Top with truffle oil and cornichons. Garnish with chives and smear of whole grain mustard.

sweet corn arepas
with chipotle pulled chicken

Serves: 8

INGREDIENTS:

- 1 ¾ cups milk
- 1 ½ cups fresh corn kernels
- 2 tablespoons unsalted butter
- 2 cups masarepa
- ¼ teaspoon Kosher salt
- 2 tablespoons unsalted butter for sautéing arepas
- ½ cup Monterey Jack cheese, shredded
- 2 chicken breasts
- 1 yellow onion, quartered
- 6-7 garlic cloves, smashed
- 1 chipotle in adobo
- 1 cup light beer
- 1 cup cilantro
- ½ cup mayonnaise
- 1 tablespoon lemon juice
- 2 garlic cloves
- chipotle hot sauce
- 1 jalapeño, thinly sliced
- ¼ cup green onion, thinly sliced

DIRECTIONS:

In a medium stock pot, add chicken breast, onion, garlic, chipotle and its adobo sauce, beer, and one cup of water. Cover and boil for 12-15 minutes. Shred and set aside. In a blender, whip cilantro, mayonnaise, lemon, and garlic. Set aside. Place the milk and the corn kernels in a blender and pulse until ground.

Pour the mixture into a saucepan and add the butter. Heat over medium heat until milk just comes to a boil. Remove from heat and let cool for 2-3 minutes. Add the masarepa to a large bowl. Slowly pour the hot milk mixture into the masarepa, stirring with a wooden spoon. Continue to stir mixture until it's cool enough to handle, then knead gently with your hands until you have a smooth dough. Season with salt to taste and knead. Shape the arepas by taking about ¼ cup of the dough and form it into a ball. Flatten between your palms into a pancake shape, smoothing cracked edges with your fingers. Flatten pancake until it's about 1/3" thick and about 1" in diameter.

Repeat with remaining dough. Melt a tablespoon of butter in a large skillet over medium-low heat. Cook the arepas in batches until golden brown and crispy on both sides, about five minutes. Place a small amount of cheese between two cakes to form like a sandwich. Warm again just to let the cheese melt. To assemble, line up the arepas, top with shredded chicken, drizzle with cilantro aioli and hot sauce. Top with jalapeño and green onions.

blueberry, ham, and swiss on brioche

Serves: 2

INGREDIENTS:

- 4 slices brioche, ½" thick
- 1 tablespoon butter, unsalted, softened
- ½ cup blueberries
- ¼ cup sugar
- 1 tablespoon lemon juice
- ¼ cup water
- 4 slices Black Forest ham, thinly sliced
- 2 slices Swiss cheese
- white truffle oil, for drizzling
- powdered sugar, for dusting

DIRECTIONS:

Preheat a flat top skillet to medium high heat. In a small stock pot, bring blueberries, sugar, lemon juice, and water to a simmer. Cook over medium heat for 10-12 minutes or until reduced by half. Set aside.

Add butter to flat top and place bread slices on it. Add ham to two bread slices, add cheese to the other two, and place a heaping spoonful of blueberry marmalade on top of the ham. After a few minutes on the flat top, and cheese has melted, fold over to make two sandwiches. Drizzle with truffle and dust with powdered sugar.

VEG FORWARD

garlic lemon butter steamed artichoke — 57

potatoes — 60

grilled whole grain crostini — 63

fried green tomatoes — 66

eggplant rollotini — 71

garlic roasted broccolini — 72

mexican street corn — 75

roasted red and green tomato casserole — 78

pan-seared shrimp — 81

roasted acorn squash — 84

sweet potato steak fries — 89

roasted tomato caprese — 92

spicy marinated cucumbers — 96

skin on roasted sweet potato — 99

couscous, sweet potato, and grilled radicchio — 102

sesame szechuan stir-fry squash — 106

roasted beets — 109

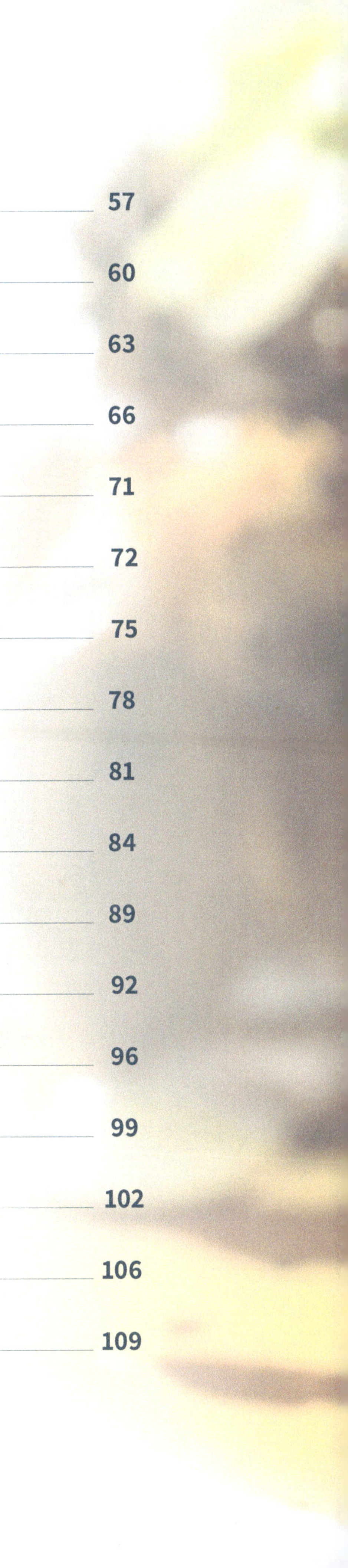

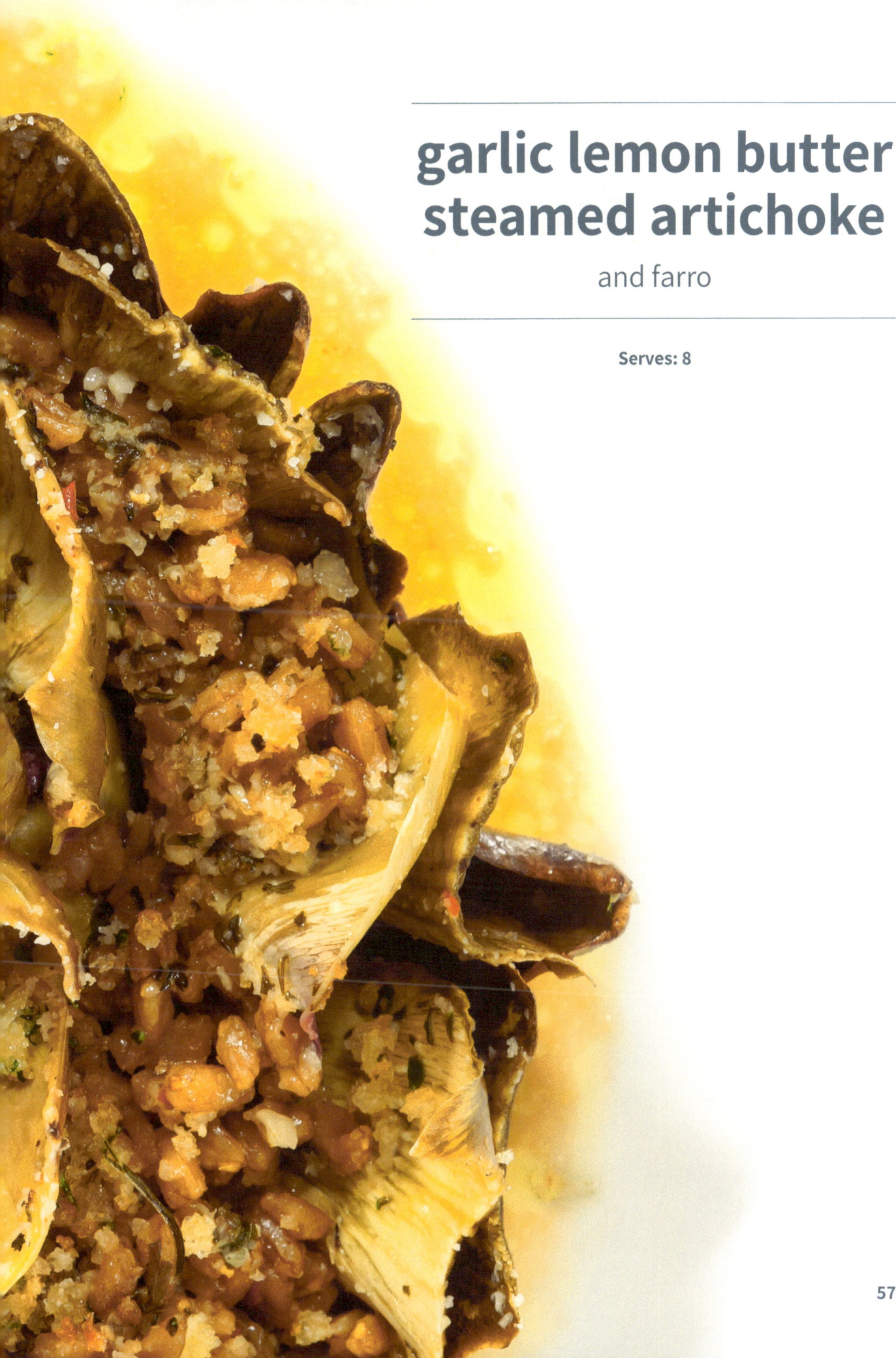

garlic lemon butter steamed artichoke
and farro

Serves: 8

INGREDIENTS:

- 1 artichoke
- ¼ cup butter, unsalted
- 1 tablespoon garlic, minced
- ¼ cup white wine
- 1 tablespoon lemon
- 1 teaspoon parsley, minced
- ¼ teaspoon crushed red pepper flakes
- 1 teaspoon thyme, pulled from stem
- Kosher salt and pepper, to taste
- 1 cup farro, cooked, steamed for 25 minutes
- lemon for finishing

DIRECTIONS:

Cut stem of artichoke and trim off the top. Cut away first outside row of artichoke leaves. Place artichoke in steamer and cook for 25 minutes. Steam artichoke until knife pierces base easily. In a large pot, add butter and garlic.

Cook for 3-4 minutes over medium high heat. Add the artichoke. Add wine and lemon juice. Cook for another three minutes.

Add parsley, crushed pepper, and thyme. Cover with lid and cook for five more minutes.

Season to taste with salt and pepper. Add cooked farro. To plate, remove the artichoke from pot and onto plate.

Spoon extra sauce all over artichoke and in between leaves. Make sure farro is spread evenly throughout the artichoke.

Sprinkle with lemon.

potatoes
with fried onions, garlic, and lemon chili

Serves: 2

INGREDIENTS:

- 2 russet potatoes, peeled and cut into chunks
- 1 small yellow onion, sliced
- 4 garlic cloves, smashed and chopped
- ¼ cup extra virgin olive oil
- 1 teaspoon canola oil
- Kosher salt
- ¼ teaspoon crushed red pepper flakes
- 1 tablespoon parsley, chopped
- 1 tablespoon lemon juice

DIRECTIONS:

Bring a small pot of salted water to a boil. Add potatoes. Boil for 12-14 minutes or until fork tender. Meanwhile, in medium frying pan heat up the olive oil and canola oil to medium high.

Add the onions. Cook for 5-7 minutes or until they begin to brown. Add the garlic, and continue cooking until garlic begins to caramelize.

Season with salt to taste. In a small bowl, combine red pepper flakes, parsley, and lemon juice.

To plate, pour fried onion and garlic over potatoes, then add the lemon chili parsley mix over it.

grilled whole grain crostini

with wine poached dried figs boursin and toasted pine nuts

Serves: 2

INGREDIENTS:

- 2 slices artisan whole grain bread, ½" thick cut
- 1 tablespoon butter, melted
- ½ cup dried black mission figs, halved
- 1 cup merlot wine
- ½ cup sugar
- ¼ cup Boursin cheese, room temperature
- 1 tablespoon pine nuts, toasted
- ¼ cup baby arugula
- extra virgin olive oil,
- Kosher salt and pepper, to taste

DIRECTIONS:

In a small stock pot, bring wine and sugar to a boil. Add the figs and lower heat to medium. Cook for ten minutes and drain. Set figs aside. On a clean work surface, place two slices of bread and using a pastry brush, brush them with melted butter.

Preheat a large pan to medium high heat. Place the butter bread onto the pan and let it sit there for 1-2 minutes or until it begins to toast around the edges. Set aside.

Spread Boursin cheese onto bread, then add the baby arugula. Drizzle with olive oil and season to taste with salt and pepper.

Add the wine poached figs and toasted pine nuts.

fried green tomatoes
with crispy hominy and blistered tomato

Serves: 2

INGREDIENTS:

- 2 green tomatoes, cut into 1/4" rings
- Kosher salt and freshly ground black pepper
- 3/4 cup all-purpose flour
- 1 tablespoon garlic powder
- 4 eggs
- 2 tablespoons milk
- 1 1/2 cups panko bread crumbs
- 1/8 teaspoon cayenne pepper
- 1/8 teaspoon paprika
- 1 cup hominy, canned and rinsed
- 1 teaspoon canola oil
- 1 teaspoon chili powder
- 1/2 teaspoon garlic salt
- 1 cup cherry tomatoes, cut in half
- 1 teaspoon lemon juice
- 1 tablespoon chives, minced
- chipotle hot sauce
- extra virgin olive oil

DIRECTIONS:

Preheat a deep fryer to 350 degrees F. Season tomatoes on both sides with salt and pepper. Place flour and garlic powder in a bowl. In another bowl, beat eggs with the milk. In another bowl, mix bread crumbs with cayenne and paprika.

Dredge tomatoes through the flour, then the eggs, and then through the bread crumbs. Add only a few pieces to the fryer and cook for about two to three minutes. Drain on paper towels and then cut in half.

Preheat the oven to 400 degrees F. Meanwhile, for the crispy hominy, toss the hominy in a bowl with oil to evenly coat.

Then add the chili powder and garlic salt. Place seasoned hominy on a baking sheet and roast in the oven for 45 minutes. In another sheet pan, place the cherry tomatoes and sprinkle with salt and olive oil. Roast for 20 minutes or until they begin to blister. In a bowl, combine crispy hominy, blistered tomatoes, lemon juice, and chives. To plate, line the cut fried tomatoes and top with hominy mixture.

Drizzle with your favorite chipotle hot sauce.

eggplant rollotini
with goat cheese and watercress

Serves: 2

INGREDIENTS:

- 1 eggplant, cut into ¼" slices lengthwise
- ¼ cup extra virgin olive oil, plus more for dressing
- 1 teaspoon garlic, minced
- Kosher salt and freshly ground pepper, to taste
- ½ cup mild goat cheese, softened
- 1 cup fresh watercress
- 1 teaspoon lemon juice
- 1 teaspoon extra virgin olive oil
- ¼ cup Parmesan shavings
- 1 tablespoon balsamic glaze

DIRECTIONS:

Preheat the grill or grill pan to medium high. On a clean work surface, place the sliced eggplant and brush with olive oil generously, then evenly spread garlic and sprinkle salt and pepper. Allow to sit for 15 minutes at room temperature. Preheat the oven to 400 degrees F. Carefully place each slice of eggplant onto the grill or grill pan, and cook for 2-3 minutes on each side. Place back onto clean work surface and allow to cool just a bit. Place a spoonful of goat cheese at the bottom of each eggplant slice and roll up. Place each rolled eggplant onto a baking dish seam side down.

Bake for 10-12 minutes. Meanwhile, place watercress in bowl. Add lemon juice, salt, and olive oil. Toss to combine. To plate, place the eggplant onto the center of a dish and top with dressed watercress and shaved Parmesan.

Drizzle with balsamic glaze.

garlic roasted broccolini

with buttered bread crumbs and lemon

Serves: 2

INGREDIENTS:

- 6 stalks broccolini, stems trimmed
- 2 tablespoons garlic slivers
- ¼ cup extra virgin olive oil
- Kosher salt and black pepper, to taste
- ¼ cup bread crumbs
- 1 teaspoon butter, unsalted
- pinch garlic salt
- ¼ cup Parmesan shavings
- 1 teaspoon lemon juice
- lemon slices, grilled as garnish

DIRECTIONS:

Preheat the oven to 425 degrees F. In a bowl, toss broccolini in garlic slivers, olive oil, salt, and pepper to evenly coat. Place on a baking dish. Roast in the oven for 12-15 minutes or until broccolini begins to brown on the edges. Meanwhile, on a small pan over medium heat toast bread crumbs with butter and garlic salt, about 1-2 minutes. When the broccolini is ready, sprinkle with buttered bread crumbs, lemon juice, and top with Parmesan shavings. Garnish with grilled lemon slices.

mexican street corn
with sofrito aioli and shaved jalapeño

Serves: 4

INGREDIENTS:

- 4 ears corn, husked
- ¼ cup unsalted butter, melted
- 1 tablespoon red bell pepper, minced
- 1 tablespoon yellow onion, minced
- 1 tablespoon garlic, minced
- 1 tablespoon olive oil
- ¼ teaspoon cumin
- 1 tablespoon tomato paste
- ¼ cup beer
- ¼ teaspoon Kosher salt
- ¼ teaspoon black pepper
- 1 tablespoon cilantro, minced
- ½ cup mayonnaise
- ½ cup Cotija cheese
- 1 teaspoon Tajín, Mexican seasoning
- 1 lime, quartered
  shaved jalapeño
  shaved radishes
  minced chives

DIRECTIONS:

Preheat oven to 450 degrees F. Slather corn with butter and place on a baking sheet. Roast in oven for 30-35 minutes. Meanwhile, make the sofrito by sautéing bell peppers, onion, and garlic in olive oil for five minutes. Add cumin and tomato paste. Stir. Add beer, salt, and pepper.

Stir and cook over medium heat for an additional five minutes. Turn off the heat and add cilantro. Set aside and allow to cool.

Once it's cooled, fold the sofrito into the mayonnaise. Allow the cooked corn to cool for a few minutes then slather the corn with sofrito aioli.

Top with Cotija cheese and sprinkle with Tajín. Add shaved jalapeño, radish, and chives. Serve with lime.

roasted red and green tomato casserole

Serves: 4

INGREDIENTS:

- 2 red tomatoes, thinly sliced
- 2 green tomatoes, thinly sliced
- 1/2 cup extra virgin olive oil
- 1/4 white balsamic vinegar
- 1/4 cup garlic, slivers
- 1 teaspoon dried oregano
- 1 tablespoon Parmesan cheese, grated
- 1 small bunch thyme
- Kosher salt, to taste
- 1/8 teaspoon crushed red pepper flakes

DIRECTIONS:

Preheat the oven to 425 degrees F. Pour olive oil in a casserole dish, spreading evenly to coat it. Add garlic slivers, sprinkle with oregano, add the thyme, and add Parmesan cheese.

Then, press the slices of tomatoes onto the pan, arranging them evenly.

Drizzle with balsamic vinegar. Season to taste with Kosher salt and sprinkle with crushed red pepper. You can add more Parmesan cheese if desired. Bake for 30-40 minutes or until tomatoes begin to brown and deepen in color.

Allow to rest for 15 minutes before slicing.

pan-seared shrimp

with pomegranate and sweet white corn pearl couscous

Serves: 2

INGREDIENTS:

- 1 lb large shrimp, peeled and deveined
- 1 tablespoon extra virgin olive oil
- 1 teaspoon lemon pepper seasoning
- 1 teaspoon paprika
- 1 cup pearled couscous, cooked to package instructions
- ½ cup white sweet corn, cooked, then cut off the husk
- ¼ cup pomegranate seeds
- 1 teaspoon jalapeño, minced, seeded
- 1 tablespoon lime juice
- Kosher salt and pepper, to taste
- ½ cup baby arugula

DIRECTIONS:

Preheat a large sauté pan to medium high heat. In a large bowl, toss shrimp in olive oil, lemon pepper, and paprika.

Add seasoned shrimp to the heated pan and cook for about two minutes per side or until shrimp begin to curl and turn opaque.

Remove from heat and set aside. In a large bowl, combine cooked couscous, corn, pomegranate, jalapeño, and lime juice.

Season to taste with salt and pepper. Add the baby arugula and toss again. To serve, place the couscous mix in the center of a dish and dot with the cooked shrimp.

roasted acorn squash
with sriracha sofrito and bleu cheese

Serves: 2

INGREDIENTS:

- 1 acorn squash, seeds removed, cut into chunks
- 1 tablespoon canola oil
- 1 teaspoon brown sugar
- ½ teaspoon garlic salt
- ½ teaspoon black pepper
- 1 tablespoon extra virgin olive oil
- 1 teaspoon yellow onion, minced
- 1 teaspoon garlic, minced
- 1 teaspoon red bell pepper, minced
- 1 teaspoon tomato paste
- 1 teaspoon cilantro, minced
- 1 tablespoon dry white wine
- 1 tablespoon Sriracha hot sauce
- Kosher salt, to taste
- ¼ cup bleu cheese
- chives, minced as garnish

DIRECTIONS:

Preheat the oven to 400 degrees F. On a clean work surface, cut the acorn squash into chunks. Toss the squash in a large bowl with canola oil to coat evenly.

Then, add brown sugar, garlic salt, and pepper. Add to a cookie sheet or baking dish and bake for 20-25 minutes until fork tender.

Meanwhile, in a small skillet, heat up olive oil to medium high heat. Add the onion, garlic, and bell peppers.

Cook for 3-5 minutes. Add the tomato paste and stir. Add cilantro and white wine.

Stir constantly. Cook for another two minutes. Season to taste with salt and pour mixture into a blender. Carefully pulse while adding Sriracha. To plate, place a heaping spoonful of the Sriracha sofrito in the center of the dish, place roasted squash around it, top with bleu cheese and chives.

sweet potato steak fries

with roasted serrano, salsa verde, and queso fresco

Serves: 2

89

INGREDIENTS:

- 1 sweet potato, cut into wedges
- canola oil, for frying
- 1 serrano pepper, seeded, deveined, chopped
- ¼ yellow onion, large chop
- 1 garlic clove
- 1 teaspoon extra virgin olive oil
- ¼ cup cilantro
- ¼ cup parsley
- 1 tablespoon lime juice
- 1 teaspoon honey
- Kosher salt and pepper, to taste
- ¼ cup queso fresco, grated

DIRECTIONS:

Preheat the oven to 375 degrees F. Preheat a fryer or large pot of canola oil to 375 degrees F. In a small bowl, toss pepper, onion, and garlic with olive oil. Place onto a baking sheet and into the oven.

Bake for 15-20 minutes and set aside. In a food processor, blend the roasted mix along with parsley, cilantro, lime juice, and honey. Season to taste with salt and pepper.

Set aside. Carefully drop the sweet potato wedges into preheated oil and fry for 4-7 minutes or until they become tender in the center.

Place steak fries onto a paper towel lined plate to drain. To plate, place fries on dish and spoon salsa verde over the top. Finish with queso fresco.

roasted tomato caprese

with garlic panzanella

Serves: 4

INGREDIENTS:

- 4 cups cherry tomatoes
- 4 cups cubed ciabatta bread
- 6 tablespoons extra virgin olive oil
- 1 teaspoon Kosher salt
- 1 teaspoon pepper
- 1 tablespoon garlic, minced
- 2 ½ cups fresh mozzarella balls
- ¼ cup red onion, shaved
- 15-20 fresh basil leaves
- ¼ Parmesan cheese, shaved
- ½ cup balsamic glaze

DIRECTIONS:

Preheat oven to 400 degrees F. On one baking sheet, lay the tomatoes down and drizzle with 1 ½ tablespoons of olive oil, ½ teaspoon salt and ½ teaspoon pepper. On a separate baking sheet, place the cubed bread and toss it with two tablespoons of olive oil and garlic.

Place both sheets in the oven. Roast the tomatoes for 20 minutes, tossing once during cooking. Toast the bread for 10-12 minutes or until golden. Place mozzarella on a paper towel to remove the moisture and water.

In a large bowl, add bread, tomatoes, onion, basil, remaining salt and pepper. Gently toss with two large spoons. Drizzle the remaining olive oil over the salad, drizzle with balsamic glaze, and top with Parmesan shavings.

spicy marinated cucumbers
with hot honey mustard

Serves: 2

INGREDIENTS:

- 1-2 cucumbers, cut into diamond shape on an angle
- 1 tablespoon white distilled vinegar
- 1 tablespoon sugar
- 1/4 teaspoon sesame oil
- 1 teaspoon crushed red pepper flakes
- 1 tablespoon Chinese hot mustard
- 1 tablespoon honey
- 1 radish, thinly sliced
- 1/8 teaspoon black sesame seeds

DIRECTIONS:

In a bowl, toss cucumbers in vinegar, sugar, sesame oil, and red pepper flakes. Cover with plastic wrap and refrigerate for four hours or overnight. In small bowl, whisk together hot mustard and honey. Set aside.

To plate, place a spoonful of marinated cucumbers in the center of a dish.

Swirl hot honey mustard around the cucumber cluster. Garnish with radish slices and sprinkle with sesame seeds.

skin on roasted sweet potato

with candied quinoa, soy brown butter, and cilantro mayo

Serves: 2

INGREDIENTS:

- 1 large sweet potato, cut into three pieces
- 2 tablespoon quinoa
- 1 tablespoon sugar
- 1 tablespoon unsalted butter
- 1 tablespoon light soy sauce
- 1 tablespoon cilantro
- 1 tablespoon mayonnaise
- ¼ teaspoon garlic, minced
- ¼ teaspoon hot sauce
- 1 tablespoon green onion, thinly sliced

DIRECTIONS:

Preheat the oven to 350 degrees F. Place cut sweet potato onto a nonstick cookie sheet. Place in oven for 15-20 minutes or until fork tender. Meanwhile, in a small pan, melt sugar and add quinoa. Cook over medium heat for 3-5 minutes until the sugar starts to turn golden.

Take off the heat and set aside. In another small pan, heat butter to medium high and cook for 2-3 minutes or until butter starts to brown. Add soy sauce and whisk vigorously to combine. Set aside. In food processor, add cilantro, mayonnaise, garlic, and hot sauce and pulse to combine. To plate, press baked sweet potatoes on the sides to push out the flesh from the top. Add a spoonful of soy brown butter to each. Top with candied quinoa and green onions. Add a dollop of cilantro mayonnaise to each piece of dressed sweet potato.

couscous, sweet potato, and grilled radicchio

Serves: 2

INGREDIENTS:

- 1 cup Israeli couscous, cooked to package instructions
- ½ cup sweet potato, small dice, roasted
- ½ radicchio
- 1-2 tablespoons extra virgin olive oil
- Kosher salt and freshly ground black pepper
- 1 teaspoon garlic, minced
- 1 tablespoon balsamic vinegar
- ½ teaspoon Dijon mustard
- ¼ teaspoon fresh thyme, removed from stemmed chives, for garnish
- balsamic glaze, or garnish

DIRECTIONS:
Preheat grill or grill pan to medium high. Brush radicchio with olive oil and sprinkle with salt and pepper to taste. Grill on all sides for 2-3 minutes on each side. In a small bowl, whisk together remaining olive oil, balsamic, mustard and thyme to make a vinaigrette.
Set aside. In a large bowl combine couscous and sweet potato. Thinly slice grilled radicchio, add to bowl, and toss. Add vinaigrette and toss. To serve, garnish with minced chives and dot with balsamic glaze.

sesame szechuan stir-fry squash

Serves: 2

INGREDIENTS:

- 1 tablespoon canola oil
- 1 yellow squash, julienned
- 1 zucchini, julienned
- 2 carrots, peeled, julienned
- 1 cup Napa cabbage, shredded
- ½ cup yellow onion, thinly sliced
- ½ cup red bell pepper, thinly sliced
- ½ cup scallion, thinly sliced lengthwise
- 1 teaspoon garlic, minced
- 1 teaspoon ginger, peeled, and grated
- ¼ cup light soy sauce
- 1 teaspoon Szechuan sauce
- ½ teaspoon sesame oil
- 1 teaspoon rice wine vinegar
- 1 teaspoon black sesame seeds

DIRECTIONS:

In a large sauté pan or wok heat canola oil over high heat. Add squash, zucchini, carrot, cabbage, onion, and bell pepper. Sauté moving frequently over high heat for 2-3 minutes.

Add garlic and ginger, cook for an additional two minutes. Add soy, Szechuan, sesame, and vinegar.

Add scallion and cook for one minute more. To plate, divide stir fry into two plates and sprinkle with black sesame seeds. Garnish with a couple of fried zucchini juliennes.

roasted beets
with goat cheese and garlic pearl couscous

Serves: 4

INGREDIENTS:

- 4 organic beets, scrubbed and washed
- 1 tablespoon canola oil
- Kosher salt and freshly ground black pepper
- 1 cup pearl couscous, cooked to package instructions
- 1 tablespoon garlic slivers
- ¼ cup extra virgin olive oil
- 1 tablespoon parsley, minced
- ¼ cup goat cheese, crumbles
- 1 tablespoon balsamic vinegar
- chives, minced for garnish
- 1 beet, cut in half

DIRECTIONS:

Preheat the oven to 350 degrees F. Rub the four beets with canola oil, and sprinkle with salt and pepper. Wrap each beer tightly with aluminum foil and bake for 1 ½ hours until fork tender. Meanwhile, take other beet and boil ½ in one cup water for 30 minutes or until liquid becomes thickened.

Take the other half and thinly slice it on a mandolin. Bake slices for 30 minutes to make beet chips. Set aside to use as garnish. After roasted beets are fork tender, unwrap and allow to sit for 45 minutes to one hour. In a small sauté pan, add olive oil over medium heat and add garlic slivers.

Cook stirring often until garlic begins to brown. Set pan aside including olive oil. Begin slicing cooked beets into ¼" thick slices. In a large bowl, combine cooked couscous, garlic and olive oil, parsley, goat cheese crumbles, and balsamic vinegar. Toss.

Top each beet ring with couscous mixture. Garnish with beet liquid, beet chips, and chives.

flat iron steak — **113**

chili-rubbed lamb tenderloin — **116**

grilled lamb chops — **119**

umami marinated skirt steak — **120**

double cut pork chop — **125**

spicy maple glazed pork tenderloin — **128**

roasted garlic ribeye — **133**

pork loin — **135**

ny strip — **139**

hoisin marinated pork tenderloin — **142**

hoisin marinated pork tenderloin — **147**

chili and summer peach pork tenderloin — **151**

seared beef — **154**

roasted bone marrow — **159**

flat iron steak

with pickled green tomato
and sweet soy glaze

Serves: 8

INGREDIENTS:

- 1   1 lb flat iron steak
- 1   tablespoon canola oil
- 1   tablespoon garlic, minced
- 3   rosemary sprigs
- ¼   cup red wine
- 1   teaspoon mustard powder
- 1   tablespoon extra virgin olive oil
-     Kosher salt and freshly ground black pepper to taste
- 1   green tomato, thinly sliced on a mandolin
- 1   cup distilled white vinegar
- ½   cup sugar, divided in half
- ½   cup light soy sauce
- 1   teaspoon corn starch slurry (corn starch diluted with water)
-     chives, minced, for garnish

DIRECTIONS:

In a large bowl, mix garlic, rosemary, wine, mustard powder, and olive oil. Place steak in a large re-sealable plastic bag and pour mixture over it. Seal tightly and refrigerate for four hours. Meanwhile, bring vinegar and ¼ cup of sugar to a boil.
Add sliced tomatoes. Cook for one minute and set aside.
In a small pot, bring soy sauce to a boil with sugar and add corn starch slurry.
Stir constantly and then set aside. Remove steak from refrigerator and also from marinade. Pat dry. Season to taste with Kosher salt and pepper. In a large skillet with canola oil on high heat, carefully add the seasoned steak.
Cook on each side 4-5 minutes or until desired doneness. Allow ten minutes to rest before slicing. Slice into ¼ inch thick pieces. Serve with pickled green tomatoes, drizzle with sweet soy, and garnish with chives.

chili-rubbed lamb tenderloin

with truffled blueberry cabernet reduction

Serves: 8

INGREDIENTS:

- 1   8-10 oz lamb tenderloin, trimmed
- 1   tablespoon chili powder
- 1   tablespoon brown sugar
- 1   teaspoon cumin
- 1   tablespoon canola oil
- 1   cup Cabernet Sauvignon
- ½   cup blueberries
- ½   cup sugar
- 1   teaspoon white truffle oil
-      chives, minced

DIRECTIONS:

On a clean work surface, season lamb tenderloin with chili powder, brown sugar, and cumin. Set aside. Heat up a large skillet with canola oil to medium high heat. Carefully place the seasoned lamb in skillet and sear on all sides for a minute each (for medium rare). Also, in a small stockpot, add Cabernet, blueberries, and sugar.

Cook down over medium heat for 12-15 minutes. Add truffle oil. To plate, slice lamb into ¼ inch thick slices. Pour sauce over and around the lamb. Garnish with minced chives.

grilled lamb chops
with pickled grapes with candied apricots

Serves: 2

INGREDIENTS:

- 1 rack New Zealand Lamb, segmented into chops
- 1 teaspoon brown sugar
- 1 teaspoon Kosher salt
- 1 teaspoon freshly ground black pepper
- canola oil
- 10-15 grapes, sliced
- 1 cup distilled vinegar
- pinch Kosher salt
- 7 dried apricots, small dice
- 1 cup water
- ¼ cup sugar
- 1 tablespoon cilantro

DIRECTIONS:

Heat up a grill pan to medium high and pour a small amount of canola oil on the bottom. On a clean work surface, lay the lamb chops and season with brown sugar, salt, and pepper. Cook on each side for 3-4 minutes. Set aside. In a small pot, bring grapes, vinegar, and salt to boil.
Cook for 7-8 minutes, strain, and set aside. In another small pot, bring water, apricots, and sugar to a boil. Cook for 10-12 minutes.
Set aside. To plate, line the lamb chops on a dish.
Top with pickled grapes and candied apricots. Finish with fresh cilantro leaves.

umami marinated skirt steak

with white corn, sweet pepper relish, and spicy soy

Serves: 2

INGREDIENTS:

- 1 lb skirt steak, trimmed
- canola oil, for coating
- 1 tablespoon white miso paste
- 1 cup water
- ½ cup corn starch
- 1 teaspoon sesame oil
- 1 tablespoon sugar
- 1 tablespoon light soy sauce
- ½ cup white corn, cooked, off the cob
- ¼ cup sweet tri-color peppers, thinly sliced
- 1 tablespoon cilantro, chopped
- 1 tablespoon lime juice
- Kosher salt and pepper to taste
- 5-6 cucumber ribbons
- ¼ cup light soy sauce
- 1 tablespoon red pepper flakes

DIRECTIONS:

In a large bowl, whisk together miso, water, corn starch, sesame, sugar, and soy sauce until everything is well combined. Add the skirt steak into mixture.

Cover and refrigerate for 2-4 hours. Meanwhile to make the white corn relish, in a small bowl, combine corn, peppers, cilantro, lime, and salt and pepper. Set aside. For the spicy soy, whisk together soy sauce and red pepper flakes. Preheat the grill or a large cast iron pan to medium high heat.

Add a small amount of canola oil just to coat. Remove the skirt steaks from marinade and pat dry. Place on the oiled grill or pan, and cook for 3-4 minutes on each side.

Allow to rest ten minutes before slicing. To plate, place sliced skirt steak on the center of the dish, then top with corn relish, and cucumber ribbons.

Finally, spoon the spicy soy sauce around the steak.

double cut pork chop
with spicy peaches and roasted hazelnuts

Serves: 2

INGREDIENTS:

- 2 double boned (16 oz) pork chops, trimmed
- 1 tablespoon brown sugar
- 1 teaspoon garlic salt
- 1 teaspoon paprika
- 1 teaspoon freshly ground black pepper
- canola oil
- ¼ cup butter, unsalted
- ½ cup peaches, thinly sliced
- 1 tablespoon brown sugar
- 1 tablespoon light soy sauce
- ¼ teaspoon crushed red pepper flakes
- ¼ cup hazelnuts, crushed
- 1 teaspoon chives, minced

DIRECTIONS:

Preheat the oven to 350 degrees F. Place the hazelnuts on a sheet pan and roast for 20 minutes. Set aside. Raise the oven temperature to 425 degrees F. Bring a large skillet with a small amount of canola oil to medium high heat. On a clean work surface, season each pork chop generously with brown sugar, garlic salt, paprika, and black pepper. Gently place pork into hot skillet, sear for 2-3 minutes on each side, and place on a baking dish. Roast in the oven for 15-20 minutes.

Meanwhile, add butter to a skillet and melt over medium high heat. Add the peaches. Cook for 1-2 minutes. Add the brown sugar and cook for another 1-2 minutes.

Add the soy sauce and red pepper flakes and reduce the heat to medium low to allow the flavors to come together. Add hazelnuts and stir in the chives. To serve, spoon the spicy peaches and hazelnuts over the pork chops. Drizzle pan sauce over the pork

spicy maple glazed pork tenderloin
with pickled red cabbage and scallion

Serves: 2

INGREDIENTS:

- 1/2 lb pork tenderloin, trimmed and cut into 1" portions
- Kosher salt and pepper
- 1 tablespoon canola oil
- 1 teaspoon cayenne pepper
- 1/4 cup pure maple syrup
- 1 cup red cabbage, shredded
- 1/2 cup red wine vinegar
- 1/4 cup sugar
- 1/8 teaspoon dried oregano
- 1/4 cup scallions, thinly sliced

DIRECTIONS:

Preheat the oven to 425 degrees F. Heat a large skillet with canola oil to medium high.

Season the pork tenderloin pieces with salt and pepper to taste.

Sear on all sides for 30 seconds and set aside. In a small stock pot, add maple syrup and cayenne pepper.

Bring to a boil and then simmer for five minutes. Cover seared pork in maple cayenne mixture.

Place on a baking dish and bake for 20 minutes. Meanwhile, using a small stock pot, simmer cabbage, vinegar, sugar, and dried oregano for 10-12 minutes. Set aside.

To plate, place the glazed pork tenderloin pieces in a line, then top with pickled cabbage, and sliced scallions. Drizzle remaining maple glaze around the plate.

roasted garlic ribeye
with fried thyme

Serves: 2

INGREDIENTS:

- 1   24 oz bone in prime ribeye, trimmed
- 1   teaspoon brown sugar
- 1   teaspoon Kosher salt
- 1   teaspoon freshly cracked black pepper
- 2   cups canola oil
- 7-8 garlic cloves, peeled
- 1   bunch fresh thyme
- 1   tablespoon cilantro

DIRECTIONS:

Preheat the oven to 500 degrees F., Rub garlic cloves with a little bit of oil and place on a baking sheet. Bake for ten minutes or until they begin to brown.

Meanwhile, remove the ribeye from refrigeration and allow to come up to room temperature.

Season with brown sugar, salt, and pepper. Set aside. In a very hot skillet with a spoonful of oil, sear seasoned ribeye 3-4 minutes on each side and place on a baking sheet.

Heat the rest of the oil in a tall medium pot to medium high. Flash fry the thyme just until moisture comes out, about ten seconds. Drain on a paper towel and set aside. Roast ribeye in oven for 10-12 minutes for medium rare, add 2 minutes for medium, and add 2 more for medium well. Remove ribeye from oven and set aside. Garnish with fried thyme and roasted garlic.

pork loin
with cognac, sage, and apple cream

Serves: 2

INGREDIENTS:

- 1/2 lb pork loin, trimmed
- Kosher salt and pepper
- 1 tablespoon canola oil
- 1 teaspoon garlic, minced
- 1 teaspoon onion, minced
- 1/8 teaspoon crushed red pepper flakes
- 3-5 sage leaves
- 1 red apple, thinly sliced
- 1 teaspoon Dijon mustard
- 1/4 cup Cognac
- 1/4 cup low sodium chicken stock
- 1/4 cup heavy cream

DIRECTIONS:

Preheat the oven to 400 degrees F. Preheat a large pan to medium high heat. Add canola oil. Season the pork generously with salt and pepper. Sear in hot pan on all sides, each side about 30-40 seconds or until it browns.

Remove pork from pan and onto a roasting pan, keeping the pan intact with all the juices, as it will be used for the sauce later.

Roast in oven for 11-14 minutes. Meanwhile, in the original searing pan, bring up heat to medium and add garlic, onion, and red pepper flakes. Cook for 1-2 minutes stirring with a wooden spoon. Add sage and apples.

Cook for another 1-2 minutes. Add sliced apples and mustard. Stir. Add Cognac and cook for one minute.

Add stock, cream, and lower to medium low heat. Cook for three minutes to allow all the flavors to come together.

Remove pork from the oven and allow to rest 10-12 minutes.
Slice pork into a few equal slices and pour sauce with apples over the sliced loin.

ny strip
with whole grain honey mustard and charred cipollini onion

Serves: 2

INGREDIENTS:

- 2   8 oz New York strip steaks
- 1   teaspoon Kosher salt
- 1   teaspoon freshly cracked black pepper
- 1   tablespoon canola oil
- ¼   cup whole grain mustard
- 1   tablespoon Dijon mustard
- ¼   honey
- ¼   cup water
- ¼   cup cipollini onions, peeled
- 1   tablespoon canola oil
- 1   cup baby arugula
- 1   tablespoon Champagne vinegar
- 1   tablespoon extra virgin olive oil
-     edible flowers, garnish

DIRECTIONS:

Preheat the oven to 500 degrees F. Season steaks with salt and pepper.

In a hot skillet or grill pan with canola oil, sear the steaks on high heat for 30 seconds on each side, then place on a baking sheet.

Finish in the oven for 6-8 minutes. Set aside. Meanwhile, in a small mixing bowl whisk together whole grain mustard, Dijon mustard, honey, and water. Set aside.

In a small sauté pan with canola oil, sauté cipollini onions over medium heat until charred in about ten minutes.

Toss arugula in Champagne vinegar and olive oil right before serving.

To plate, slice steaks into 1/4 inch thick slices. Drizzle with honey mustard, and add charred cipollini onions.

Top with dressed arugula and garnish with edible flowers.

hoisin marinated pork tenderloin

with plum relish and plum sauce

Serves: 2

INGREDIENTS:

- 1 lb pork tenderloin, trimmed, cut into four equal pieces
- ½ cup hoisin sauce
- ½ cup light soy sauce
- ½ cup sweet chili sauce
- 1 tablespoon garlic, minced
- 2 plums, cored, small dice
- ½ white onion, minced
- ¼ cup cilantro, minced
- 1 teaspoon jalapeño, seeded, deveined, minced
- Kosher salt and freshly ground pepper, to taste
- 1 tablespoon lime juice
- 1 tablespoon honey
- ¼ cup plum sauce
- cooking spray

DIRECTIONS:

In a large bowl, whisk together hoisin sauce, soy sauce, sweet chili sauce, and garlic.

Add the pork tenderloin pieces. Cover and refrigerate for 4-6 hours.

In a small bowl, combine plums, onion, cilantro, jalapeño, salt, pepper, lime juice, and honey. Set aside.

This step can be done earlier and refrigerated.
Preheat the oven to 425 degrees F.
Remove pork from marinade and allow to sit at room temperature for 30 minutes.
Spray a large baking dish and place pork in it.
Bake for 17-25 minutes or until cooked through.
To serve, top each piece of pork with plum relish and drizzle plum sauce around it.

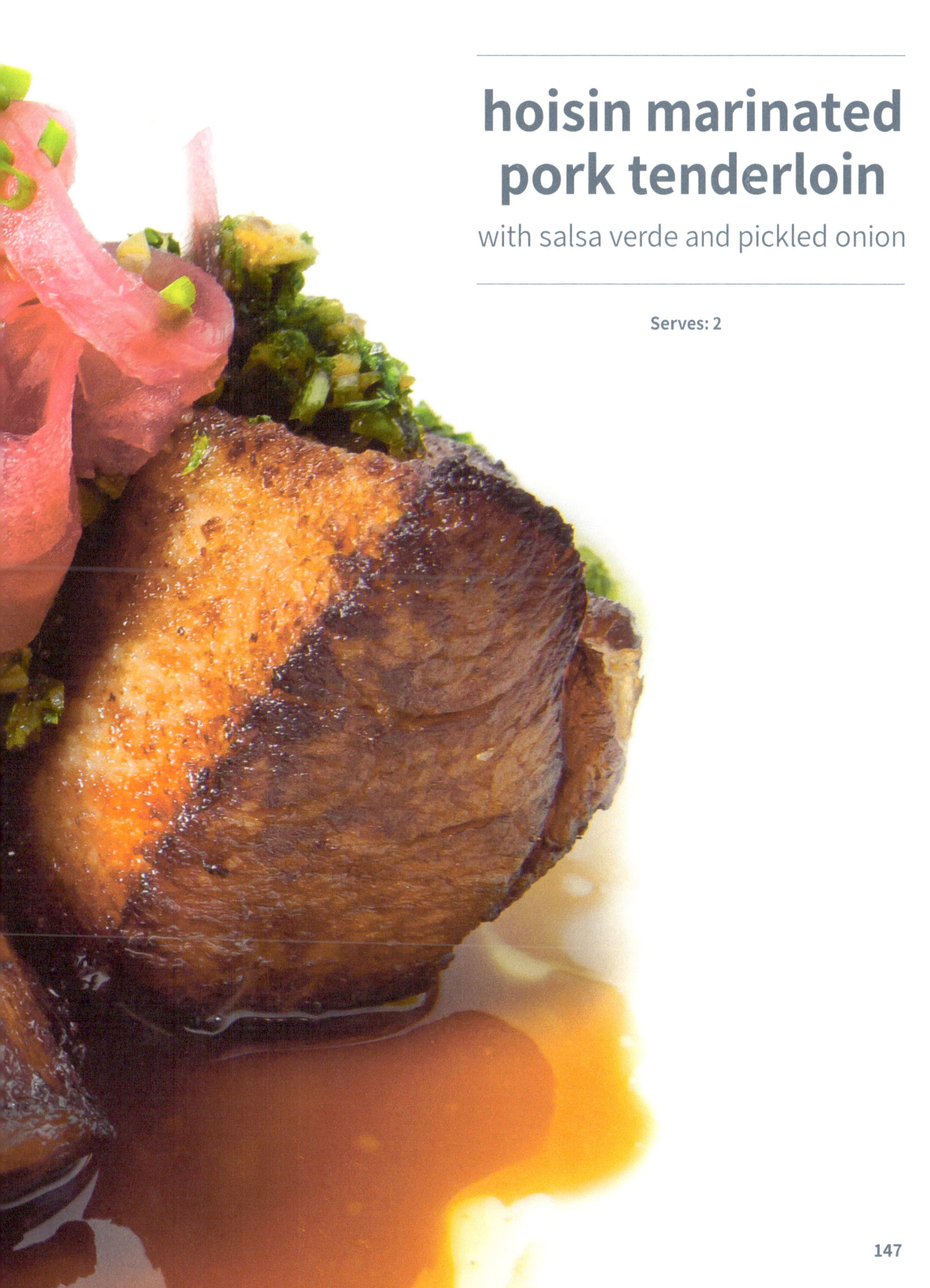

hoisin marinated pork tenderloin
with salsa verde and pickled onion

Serves: 2

INGREDIENTS:

- ¼ lb pork tenderloin, trimmed
- ½ cup hoisin sauce
- ½ cup rice wine vinegar
- ½ cup honey
- 1 tablespoon garlic, minced
- 2 tomatillos, cleaned and husked
- ½ jalapeño, seeded and stemmed
- ¼ cup cilantro, chopped
- 1 tablespoon onion, chopped
- 1 tablespoon lime
- ¼ teaspoon Kosher salt
- ¼ cup red onion, thinly sliced
- ¼ cup red wine vinegar
- 1 tablespoon sugar
- pinched dried oregano

DIRECTIONS:

On a clean work surface, cut pork tenderloin into 1 ½" diagonal wedges. Whisk hoisin, vinegar, honey, and garlic to create a marinade.
Add pork and marinade for four hours.
Meanwhile for the salsa verde, roughly chop the tomatillos and the jalapeño. In a food processor, combine the tomatillos, jalapeno, cilantro, onion, lime, and salt.
Process to a coarse purée and set aside.
In a small pan, simmer red onion, vinegar, sugar, and oregano for five minutes. Set aside.
Preheat the oven to 475 degrees F.
Remove the pork from the marinade, pat dry, and place on a baking sheet. Bake for 12-15 minutes. Top pork with salsa verde and pickled onions.

chili and summer peach pork tenderloin

Serves: 2

INGREDIENTS:

- ½ lb pork tenderloin, trimmed, cut into ½" medallions
- ½ cup light soy sauce
- 1 tablespoon Chinese hot mustard
- 1 tablespoon garlic, minced
- 1 tablespoon cilantro, chopped
- ½ cup honey
- 1 tablespoon sesame oil
- 1 tablespoon canola oil
- 1 peach, sliced
- ¼ cup bell pepper, sliced
- 1 teaspoon jalapeño, thinly sliced
- 1 teaspoon Anaheim chili, thinly sliced
- ¼ cup sweet chili sauce
- 1 tablespoon chives, minced

DIRECTIONS:

In a large bowl, whisk soy sauce, mustard, garlic, cilantro, honey, and sesame oil to make a marinade.

Add pork, cover, and refrigerate for 3-4 hours.

Preheat the oven to 425 degrees F.

Remove pork from marinade and place on a cookie sheet.

Roast for 12-14 minutes. In a large skillet over medium high heat, add canola oil, peach, peppers, chilis, and sweet chili sauce.

When it comes to a simmer add the pork and cook for an additional 4-5 minutes.

Add chives and serve.

seared beef

with fried garlic, onions, and alfalfa sprouts

Serves: 2

INGREDIENTS:

- ½ lb beef tenderloin, trimmed and cut into 1" chunks
- Kosher salt and freshly ground black pepper, to taste
- ¼ cup canola oil
- ½ cup yellow onion, chopped
- ¼ cup garlic, chopped
- ¼ teaspoon garlic parsley salt
- ¼ teaspoon crushed red pepper flakes
- 1 tablespoon lemon juice
- ¼ cup parsley, chopped
- ½ cup alfalfa sprouts
- hot sauce, for garnish

DIRECTIONS:

On a clean work surface, season beef with salt and pepper.

Preheat a large skillet to medium high heat and add canola oil.

Carefully add the seasoned beef chunks to hot oil. Do not move until it has seared for two minutes. Repeat for each side. Remove beef from skillet and reduce heat to medium low. Add onion.

Cook for 2-3 minutes. Add garlic and parsley. Cook for another 2-3 minutes. Season with garlic salt and red pepper flakes.

Stir in lemon juice. To serve, place the fried onion and garlic mix on a plate, add seared beef, and top with alfalfa sprouts.

Garnish with a drizzle of hot sauce.

roasted bone marrow

with chimichurri and pickled onions

Serves: 2

159

INGREDIENTS:

- 3   3" tall veal bone marrow bones
- 1   cup veal stock
- ¼   cup tomato paste
- ¼   cup garlic, minced
- ¼   teaspoon dried oregano
- ¼   teaspoon crushed red pepper flakes
- 1   cup dry red wine
- 1   shallot, minced
- 1   Fresno chile, minced
- 1   tablespoon garlic, minced
- ½   cup red wine vinegar
- 1   teaspoon Kosher salt, plus more
- ½   cup cilantro, chopped
- ¼   cup flat-leaf parsley, chopped
- 1   tablespoon fresh oregano, chopped
- ¾   cup extra virgin olive oil
- ½   cup red onion, thinly sliced
- 1   cup red wine vinegar
- ½   cup sugar
-     rustic buttered toasted bread

DIRECTIONS:

Preheat the oven to 350 degrees F. Place the bones in a baking dish. In a large bowl, whisk together stock, tomato paste, garlic, oregano, red pepper, and wine. Pour over bones and into the baking dish. Cover tightly with a aluminum foil and bake for 1 ½ hours. Meanwhile, in another large bowl mix shallot, chile, garlic, vinegar, salt, herbs, and olive oil. Set aside. In a small stock pot, bring red onions, vinegar, and sugar to a boil. Once it reaches a boil, turn off heat and set aside.

To serve, place bone marrow bones on a plate, spoon chimichurri on top, and finish with pickled onions and toasts.

DESSERTS

blueberry pastry tart	**164**
profiteroles	**168**
lemon pie	**170**
cookies and cream ice cream pie	**174**
rice crispies key lime	**179**
bananas foster	**182**
crispy nutella stuffed wontons	**187**
blueberry, white chocolate, pecan cookie cake	**190**
s'mores cheesecake	**195**

blueberry pastry tart

Serves: 8

INGREDIENTS:

2	cups all-purpose flour
2	tablespoons sugar
1	teaspoon Kosher salt
1	cup unsalted butter
¼	cup milk
2	cups blueberries
1	cup water
1	cup sugar
2	eggs, beaten
1	cup powdered sugar
1	tablespoon milk
¼	teaspoon vanilla extract

DIRECTIONS:

In the food processor combine the flour, sugar, and salt. Dice the cold butter into small ½" pieces and add to the flour mixture. Pulse it several times. Add the milk. Pulse until dough forms.

Turn the dough out onto a piece of plastic wrap and wrap tightly, then chill for at least two hours. Combine the blueberries, water, and sugar. Cook over low heat stirring often for about 20 minutes until a sauce-like compote is achieved. Refrigerate. For the dough, knead it with extra flour to get it to a roll-able consistency.

Preheat the oven to 375 degrees F. Roll the dough to less than ¼" thick.

Cut out rectangles that are about 3" x 4 ½"

Fill half of the rectangles of dough with two tablespoons of blueberry filling.

Cover with another rectangle of dough and with a fork, crimp the edges to seal. Brush each tart with beaten eggs and bake for 18-20 minutes or until golden brown.

Cool for 15 minutes. Meanwhile, whisk together powdered sugar, milk, and vanilla to make glaze. Drizzle over each tart.

profiteroles

with pistachio gelato and dark chocolate ganache

Serves: 4

INGREDIENTS:

- ½ cup water
- ½ stick unsalted butter
- ½ teaspoon Kosher salt
- 1 tablespoon sugar
- ½ cup all-purpose flour
- 2 eggs
- ¾ cup unsalted shelled pistachios
- 1 cup sugar
- 2 cups whole milk
- 1 teaspoon almond extract
- 5 large egg yolks
- 2 drops green food coloring
- 1 cup heavy cream
- 1 cup semi sweet chocolate chips
- 1 cup dark chocolate chips
- powdered sugar, for garnish

DIRECTIONS:
For the gelato, finely grind one cup pistachios and 1/4 cup sugar in processor. Combine pistachio mixture, milk, and almond extract in heavy saucepan. Bring to boil. Whisk yolks and ½ cup sugar in large bowl to blend. Gradually whisk milk mixture into yolk mixture. Return mixture to saucepan. Stir over medium-low heat for about ten minutes or until custard thickens. Remove from heat. Whisk in food coloring. Refrigerate custard until cold, about 2-3 hours. Process custard in ice cream maker according to manufacturer's instructions. Transfer to covered container and freeze until ready for use.
Preheat the oven to 425 degrees F.
In a small saucepan combine the water, butter, salt, sugar, and bring to a boil. Reduce the heat and add the flour all at once and stir it vigorously with a wooden spoon.

Cook for about 1-2 minutes or until the mixture has formed a ball, has a slightly sweaty look to it, and it has pulled away from the pan.
Transfer the mixture to a mixing bowl and let cool for five minutes. Using an electric mixer, beat in the eggs, one egg at a time. Transfer the mixture to a pastry bag equipped with a large straight tip and pipe 1" balls onto a sheet pan lined with parchment paper. When done dip your finger in water and smooth the top of each ball. Bake in the preheated oven for 20 to 25 minutes, rotating the tray halfway through the cooking time to insure even cooking. Cool for ten minutes. When ready to serve, cut in half horizontally and fill with pistachio gelato. For the ganache, heat cream in a small sauce pan to a simmer. Place chocolate chips in a bowl. Pour hot cream over chocolate chips and whisk until smooth. Drizzle ganache over each gelato-filled profiterole and dust with powdered sugar.
Fork, crimp the edges to seal. Brush each tart with beaten eggs and bake for 18-20 minutes or until golden brown.
Cool for 15 minutes. Meanwhile, whisk together powdered sugar, milk, and vanilla to make glaze. Drizzle over each tart.

lemon pie
with brown sugar meringue

Serves: 8

INGREDIENTS:

- 1 1/2 cups graham cracker crumbs
- 1/3 cup sugar
- 1/4 cup unsalted butter, melted
- 4 large egg yolks (reserve the whites for the meringue)
- 1 14 oz can sweetened condensed milk
- 1 teaspoon packed finely grated lemon zest, from one lemon
- 1/2 cup fresh lemon juice
- 4 large egg whites
- 6 tablespoons brown sugar
- 1/2 teaspoon vanilla extract
- 1/4 teaspoon cream of tartar

DIRECTIONS:

Preheat the oven to 375 degrees F. In a medium bowl, mix together the graham cracker crumbs and sugar. Add the melted butter and stir, then work it with your hands until the mixture is well combined. Using your fingers and the bottom of a clean drinking glass or measuring cup, press the crumbs firmly into the bottom and up the sides of a 9" pie pan. Bake for about ten minutes, until slightly browned. Set aside to cool for ten minutes.

In a medium bowl, whisk together the egg yolks, sweetened condensed milk, lemon zest, and lemon juice. Pour into the warm crust. Lower the oven heat to 325 degrees F.

Bring about ½" of water to a simmer in a pot that's large enough to hold the bowl of a stand mixer without letting it touch the water. Reduce the heat to low.

Put the egg whites and sugar in the bowl turn off the heat and whisk until frothy. Put the bowl over the pot and whisk vigorously until the whites are very warm to the touch. Remove the bowl from the heat and transfer it to the stand mixer fit with the whisk attachment.

Add the vanilla and cream of tartar. Beat over medium high speed for five minutes or until the egg whites form thick, glossy, medium-firm peaks. Mound the meringue onto the wet lemon filling.

Using a wooden spoon, spread the meringue over the entire surface of the filling, making sure to go all the way to the edge. Bake for about 20 minutes, or until the meringue is lightly browned.

Let the pie cool completely and refrigerate.

cookies and cream ice cream pie

with chocolate ganache

Serves: 10

INGREDIENTS:

- 30-40 chocolate sandwich cookies, such as Oreos, crushed
- 1 prepared chocolate pie crust
- ½ cup cool whip topping
- ½ cup cream cheese, softened
- 3 ½ cups vanilla ice cream
- 1 teaspoon vanilla extract
- ½ semi-sweet chocolate chips
- ½ cup heavy cream
- vanilla ice cream for serving

DIRECTIONS:

In a mixer using the paddle attachment, whip together crushed cookies, whip topping, cream cheese, vanilla extract, and vanilla ice cream for 30 seconds. Press mixture down onto chocolate pie crust. Press down evenly to make sure there are no air pockets.

Cover with plastic wrap and freeze for 2-3 hours. For the ganache, place chocolate chips in a small bowl. Heat heavy cream to simmer and then pour over chocolate chips.

Let it sit for a few seconds then whisk to combine. Set aside. For serving, cut a slice of the pie, add a scoop of ice cream if desired, and pour chocolate ganache over pie and around the plate.

rice crispies key lime

with toasted marshmallow and blackberries

Serves: 8

INGREDIENTS:

- 1 cup puffed rice cereal
- 1/2 cup puffed rice cereal marshmallow treat, chopped
- 1/4 cup sugar
- 1/8 teaspoon cinnamon
- 1/2 cup melted butter, unsalted
- 2 14 oz cans condensed milk
- 2 eggs
- 1 cup key lime juice, fresh
- 1 cup marshmallow fluff
- 15-20 blackberries, fresh
- powdered sugar
- mint leaves, garnish

DIRECTIONS:

Preheat the oven to 325 degrees F. In a bowl, mix rice cereal, marshmallow treats, sugar, cinnamon, and butter.

Press onto a greased 8x8 baking dish and bake for ten minutes, then allow to cool. In a blender, whip condensed milk, key lime, and egg until well combined.

Pour mixture onto baked crust. Lower oven temperature to 300 and place key lime pie in a water bath. Bake for 12-15 minutes.

Allow to cool. Refrigerate for 4-6 hours to allow to set. To serve, place a dollop of marshmallow fluff on each serving and torch it. Then add fresh blackberries, powdered sugar, and a mint leaf.

bananas foster
with crunchy oat topping

Serves: 4

INGREDIENTS:

- ¼ cup unsalted butter
- 1 cup brown sugar
- pinch Kosher salt
- ½ teaspoon cinnamon
- ¼ cup banana liqueur
- 4 bananas, cut in half lengthwise, then halved
- ¼ cup dark rum
- 4 scoops vanilla ice cream

TOPPING:

- ½ cup unsalted butter
- 1 cup brown sugar
- ¾ cup all-purpose flour
- ¾ cup oatmeal
- ½ teaspoon cinnamon
- ¼ teaspoon Kosher salt

DIRECTIONS:

Preheat the oven to 400 degrees F. Make the crunchy oat topping first by combining butter, brown sugar, flour, oatmeal, cinnamon, and salt in a bowl. Use a pastry cutter or forks until mixture resembles coarse crumbs.

Place on a parchment paper-lined sheet pan and bake for 20 minutes or until golden brown.

Set aside. For the Bananas Foster, combine the butter, sugar, salt, and cinnamon in a large sauté pan and cook over medium low heat until sugar dissolves.

Stir in the banana liqueur, then place the bananas in the pan. When the banana sections soften and begin to brown, carefully add the rum.

Continue to cook the sauce until the rum is hot, then tip the pan slightly to ignite the rum.

When the flames subside, lift the bananas out of the pan and place four pieces over each portion of ice cream. Spoon sauce over the top of the ice cream and add crunchy oat topping.

crispy nutella stuffed wontons
with crème anglaise

Serves: 2-3

INGREDIENTS:

- 6   2x2" wonton wrappers, cut diagonally to make 12 triangles
- 1   egg, beaten
- ½   cup Nutella
-      canola oil, for frying
- 1   tablespoon powdered sugar, for dusting
- ½   cup whole milk
- ½   cup heavy cream
- 1   vanilla bean, split
- 1   teaspoon vanilla extract
- 3   large egg yolks
- 3   tablespoons sugar

DIRECTIONS:

Preheat a large pot with canola oil to 350 degrees F. or medium high heat.

On a clean work surface, lay out six wonton triangles. Then spoon a nickel sized amount of Nutella onto the center of the triangle, making sure not to touch the edges.

Dip index finger into beaten egg and cover the edges of the triangle with the beaten egg. Lay another wonton triangle over the top, press, and seal the edges. Repeat the remaining five.

Set aside. Meanwhile, to make the crème anglaise, combine milk and heavy cream in medium saucepan. Scrape in seeds from vanilla bean and add it to the cream mixture. Bring crema mixture to simmer.

Remove from heat. Add the vanilla extract. Whisk egg yolks and sugar in medium bowl to blend. Gradually whisk hot mixture into yolk mixture.

Return custard to saucepan. Stir over low heat until custard thickens and leaves path on back of spoon when finger is drawn across, about 5-7 minutes.

Strain and set aside. Slowly dip each assembled wonton into hot oil and allow to fry for two minutes on each side or until golden brown.

Place on a paper towel lined plate to drain. To serve, dust with powdered sugar, then drizzle with extra Nutella and crème anglaise.

blueberry, white chocolate, pecan cookie cake

Serves: 4

INGREDIENTS:

- 4 tablespoons butter, room temperature and soft
- 1/2 cup packed brown sugar
- 1 tablespoon vanilla extract
- 1 large egg
- 1 cup all-purpose flour
- 1/2 teaspoon baking powder
- 1/8 teaspoon Kosher salt
- 1/3 cup white chocolate chips
- 1/2 cup blueberries
- 1/4 cup pecans, chopped
- powdered sugar, for dusting

DIRECTIONS:

Preheat the oven to 350 degrees F.
In a medium size bowl, cream butter and brown sugar with an electric mixer. Add vanilla and egg and mix until smooth. In another bowl, combine flour, baking powder, and salt. Add to mixing bowl and mix until well incorporated. Fold in white chocolate chips, blueberries, and pecans. Place dough onto a plastic wrap-lined cutting board.
Wrap tightly and refrigerate for 2-3 hours. Using a greased muffin tin, place a large scoop of the dough onto each muffin slot.
Bake cookies for 12-15 minutes. Allow to cool for 10-15 minutes. Flip over and dust with powdered sugar.

s'mores cheesecake

Serves: 8-10

INGREDIENTS:

- 2   8 oz packages cream cheese, softened
- 1/2   cup sugar
- 1   tablespoon vanilla extract
- 2   eggs, beaten
- 1   cup graham cracker crumbs, plus more for garnish
- 1/4   cup unsalted butter, melted
- 1/8   teaspoon cinnamon
- 1   cup marshmallow fluff
- 1/4   cup dark chocolate
- cooking spray

DIRECTIONS:

Preheat the oven to 325 degrees F. In a mixing bowl, combine graham cracker crumbs, butter, and cinnamon.

Spray a cheesecake pan (springform pan) or pie pan with nonstick spray. Press the graham mixture evenly onto the bottom of the pan.

Bake for ten minutes, remove from the oven, and allow to cool.

Meanwhile, beat cream cheese, sugar, vanilla, and eggs until well incorporated and smooth.

Pour mixture onto baked crust. Bake for 40-45 minutes and then refrigerate for 4-6 hours to allow to set. To plate, use a scooper to create cheesecake balls, top with a piece of chocolate and a dollop of marshmallow. Torch the marshmallow and then garnish with extra graham crumbs and melted chocolate.

fundamentals

WHY BRINE A CHICKEN BEFORE COOKING?

It will make your chicken taste that much better.

The most basic brine is just saltwater. Half a cup to one cup of salt per gallon of water. Dissolve the salt, submerge the bird in the brine for a couple of hours to overnight, then dry and roast. It will be much juicier and flavorful than an unbrined bird. A brine can also bring extra flavors to the party. Try using tea or whiskey instead of water. Spice it up using crushed peppercorns, allspice berries, juniper berries, dried chiles, lemons, or whatever else sounds good. Osmosis will carry the flavored liquid into the meat.

MY FAVORITE POULTRY BRINE RECIPES:

MAPLE WHISKEY BRINE

INGREDIENTS:

- 3 cups whiskey
- 3 cups maple syrup
- 1 cup Kosher salt
- 3 tablespoons black peppercorns
- 7 bay leaves
- 8 cloves garlic, minced
- 4 sprigs fresh rosemary
- 5 sprigs fresh thyme
- peel of 3 large oranges, cut into large strips
- peel of 2 red apples
- peel of 2 green apples
- 2 quarts ice water

Directions:
Combine the whiskey, maple syrup, salt, peppercorns, bay leaves, garlic, rosemary, thyme, orange peel, apple peel, and two quarts of ice water in a large pot. Bring to a boil, stirring to dissolve the salt, then turn off the heat and cover. Allow to cool completely.

SWEET TEA BRINE

INGREDIENTS:

- 2 lemons
- 1 quart very strong tea
- 1 cup sugar
- ½ cup Kosher salt
- ¼ cup black peppercorns
- 1 quart ice water

Directions:
To make the brine, zest, then slice the lemons. Put the lemon zest and slices in a saucepan. Add the tea, sugar, and salt. Simmer the mixture over medium-high heat until the salt and sugar dissolve. Add peppercorns. Add one quart of ice water.

BEST PASTA DOUGH FROM SCRATCH

INGREDIENTS:

- 3 large eggs, beaten
- 2 cups all-purpose flour
- 1 tablespoon extra virgin olive oil
- 1 teaspoon Kosher salt

Directions:

Mix eggs, flour, oil, and salt in the bowl of a stand mixer with your hands until a loose dough forms. Knead with dough hook until dough is smooth and elastic, about 10-12 minutes. Cover dough with plastic wrap and let rest at least 30 minutes to one hour. Cut and roll as desired.

HOMEMADE CHICKEN BROTH

INGREDIENTS:

- 3 roasting chickens
- 3 large yellow onions, unpeeled and quartered
- 6 carrots, unpeeled and halved
- 6 stalks celery with leaves, cut into chunks
- 20 sprigs fresh parsley
- 15 sprigs fresh thyme
- 20 sprigs fresh dill
- 2 heads garlic, unpeeled and cut in half
- 2 tablespoons Kosher salt
- 2 teaspoons whole black peppercorns
- 5 bay leaves
- 7 quarts water

Directions:

Place the chickens, onions, carrots, celery, parsley, thyme, dill, garlic, and seasonings in a 16 to 20-quart stockpot. Add seven quarts of water and bring to a boil. Simmer, uncovered, for four hours. Strain through a colander and discard the solids. Chill the stock overnight. The next day, remove the surface fat.

HOMEMADE CHIPOTLE HOT SAUCE:

INGREDIENTS:

- 16 medium tomatillos, husks removed and rinsed
- 7 cloves garlic, unpeeled and lightly crushed
- 3 tablespoons ground New Mexico chiles
- 2 teaspoons ground cumin
- 2 teaspoons lime zest
- 2 tablespoons lime juice
- 1 teaspoon Kosher salt
- ½ teaspoon black pepper

Directions:

Preheat oven to broil. Line a baking sheet with aluminum foil.
Place the tomatillos and crushed garlic on the baking sheet and place in oven. Broil until charred, about 12-15 minutes, flipping halfway through. Peel garlic. In a food processor, combine tomatillos, garlic, ground chiles, cumin, lime zest and juice, one teaspoon salt, and ½ teaspoon pepper. Process until the mixture is smooth.

QUICK STEAK SAUCE

INGREDIENTS:

- 3 tablespoons ketchup
- 1 tablespoon Worcestershire sauce
- ½ teaspoon light soy sauce
- ¼ teaspoon onion powder
- ¼ teaspoon garlic powder
- ¼ teaspoon red wine vinegar
- 3 dashes hot sauce

Directions:

In a mixing bowl, whisk together all of the ingredients.